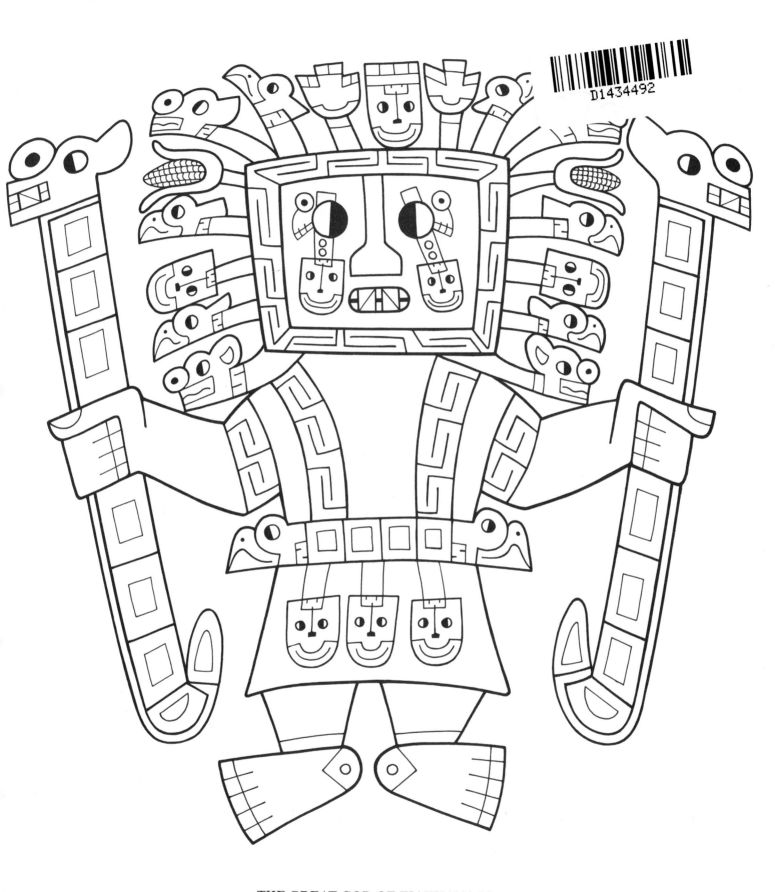

THE GREAT GOD OF TIAHUANACO

The Incas worshipped the sun more than any other god, and in the time of the Incas this was thought
to be the sun, his head surrounded by rays. But, this picture and stone carvings like it were made
long before the Incas. It was probably intended to be the supreme creator god, Viracocha.

From a stone relief in the ruins of Chavín de Huantar, Peru. A.D. 200-400.

A JAGUAR GOD AND SNAKES

From a Chimú gold sacrificial knife found near Lambayeque. Museo Nacional de Arqueología, Lima.

THE GOD-KING NAYMLAP

He brought the Yuncas or plains dwellers to their homes on a fleet of balsa-rafts. The Yuncas cultivated the desert with great irrigation systems, but they were in time defeated by the Incas.

From a Mochica pottery vessel in the Museum für Völkerkunde, Berlin. A.D. 500-800.

A RUNNING FOX GOD

From a Mochica pottery vessel.
Museum für Völkerkunde,
Berlin. A.D. 500-800.

A MOCHICA MESSENGER

The Mochicas did not have a system of writing like ours. It is possible, however, that they used lima beans to communicate. Designs carved on beans may have been read by trained readers. Many Mochica vases show runners holding bags, with beans all around them. These are thought to be messengers carrying bags of beans to be read.

From a Mochica pottery jar from the northwest coast of Peru; Museum für Völkerkunde, Munich.

THE MOON-GOD TRAVELLING OVER THE SEA IN A REED BOAT

The jars along the side of the boat may contain dew, which was believed to be brought by the moon-god. In the dry land on the coast every bit of moisture was precious, including the dew which helped seeds to sprout.

From a Mochica pottery vessel.
Trujillo, Peru. A.D. 500-800.

MOCHICA WARRIORS

About A.D. 400-1000 the northern coast of Peru was inhabited by people called the Mochica. They left thousands of pieces of pottery decorated with pictures like this. From them we can see what the Mochica looked like and what sorts of gods they worshipped.

CÕTADOR·MAIOR·I·TE3ORERO
TAVANTINSVIO·QVIPOC
CVRACA·CON DOR·CHAVA

From the *Nueva Corónica y Buen Gobierno,* a Peruvian codex compiled by Felipe Guamán Poma de Ayala about 1613. Royal Library, Copenhagen.

From a Mochica painted vase from Huaca de la Campana, Pampa de Yaguey, Northern Peru. A.D. 400-600. Museo Nacional de Arqueología, Lima.

A QUIPUCAMAYOC WITH QUIPU AND ABACUS

The Incas had no system for writing words or numbers. Nevertheless, they were able to keep complex records by use of the *quipu,* a form of tally made up of strings knotted in particular ways. Calculations were made on a sort of abacus like that in the left-hand corner; then numbers were recorded on the *quipu.* Thus records of taxes paid, the contents of storehouses or even the verses of poems were accessible to the *quipu*-interpreter or *quipucamayoc.*

A MOCHICA MUSICIAN PLAYING A PAN PIPE

From a Mochica pottery vessel.
Trujillo, Peru. A.D. 500-800.

The great Inca Empire existed for less than 100 years before its conquest in 1533. It extended several hundred miles inland along most of the western coast of South America. The emperor was named the Inca; this is a picture of the 11th Inca, HUAYNA CAPAC, who brought the empire to its greatest extent. By the time he died, however, the Spanish had already landed, and the 12th Inca was the last. Under the Inca, nobles and priest directed the people in their use of land and llamas, almost all of which were owned by the Inca. Land for growing food was allotted yearly according to the size of the family, and every man provided the Inca with a certain amount of labor every year.

A MOCHICA WARRIOR

EL ONZENOINGA
GVAINACAPAC

XIUHTECUTLI, THE FIRE GOD, AT THE NAVEL OF THE EARTH

From him grow the four world directional trees. East is on the top of the picture, the place of the rising sun from whence arose QUETZALCOATL. Here ITZLI, the god of the sharp stone, faces the god of the rising sun. North is to the right where CINCEOTL, the corn god, faces MICTLANTECUHTLI, the god of the dead. West is on the bottom; here XOCHIQUETZAL, the goddess of flowers, faces a goddess of drunkenness and witchcraft. South, on the left, THALOC, the rain god, faces a god of the underworld. It is a world of opposites. East and west are reversed, it has been suggested, because this is a night-time vision.

From the Codex Magliabecchi,
Biblioteca Nazionale Centrale,
Florence. Aztec.

**QUETZALCOATL, GOD OF THE
MORNING STAR AND OF THE RISING SUN,
DWELLS IN THE WEST**

Ehecatl, the god of wind, was interchangeable with Quetzalcoatl.

**AN OWL REPRESENTING
THE MOON ON THE
PYRAMID OF THE NORTH**

From a Huaxtec relief from Tepetzintla. Museo Nacional de Antropología, Mexico City.

QUETZALCOATL AS VENUS, THE EVENING STAR

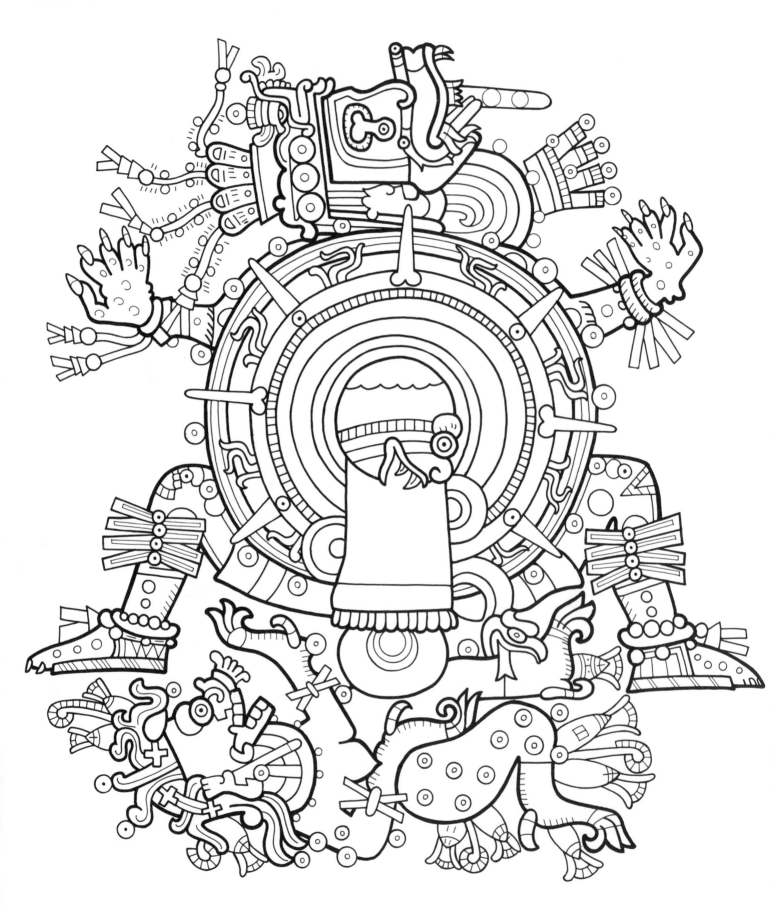

XOLOTL, THE DOG GOD OF THE EVENING STAR, THE TWIN OF QUETZALCOATL

A GODDESS OF DEATH

From the Codex Magliabecchi;
Biblioteca Nazionale Centrale,
Florence. Aztec.

THE FESTIVAL OF XOCHIHUITL IN HONOR OF MACUILXOCHITL, THE GOD OF MUSIC AND DANCING, GAMES AND PLEASURE, AND AN ASPECT OF XOCHIPILLI, THE GOD OF FLOWERS AND BEAUTY, LOVE AND HAPPINESS

The man in front is playing a shell trumpet.

EHECATL, THE GOD OF WIND

AN EAGLE KNIGHT, A WARRIOR OF HUITZILOPOCHTLI, THE GOD OF THE SUN AND WAR

A JAGUAR GLADIATOR
Jaguar knights were warriors of TEZCATLIPOCA, the Lord of the Smoking Mirror, a God of Fire, the Wizard God.

From the Codex Fejérváry-Mayer, City Museum, Liverpool. Mixtec.

XOCHIQUETZAL, THE GREAT MOTHER EARTH, AND XOCHIPILLI, THE GOD OF FLOWERS AND BEAUTY, LOVE AND HAPPINESS

From an Aztec shield covered with feathers;
Museum für Völkerkunde, Vienna.
A.D. 1486-1503.

A COYOTE, THE SYMBOL OF THE CRUEL AZTEC EMPEROR, AHUITZOTL

A Meeting of Maya Merchants. From a painted vase from Chama, Guatemala highlands; University Museum, Philadelphia. Late Classic period, Chama 3, A.D. 750-900.

From a statue found near the Pyramid of the Moon, Teotihuacan. Classic, Teotihuacan III, A.D. 350-650. Museo Nacional de Antropología, Mexico City.

CHALCHIUTLICUE, LADY OF THE JADE SKIRT, THE WATER GODDESS OF TEOTIHUACAN

Teotihuacan was a vast city in the Valley of Mexico dedicated solely to the gods. The huge pyramids of the Sun and the Moon may still be seen there. Teotihuacan greatly influenced the Maya cities to the south.

From a painted vase from
Ratinlinxul, Guatemala highlands;
University Museum, Philadelphia.
Late Classic period, Chama 3,
A.D. 750-900.

A TRAVELLING GENTLEMAN FROM RATINLINXUL

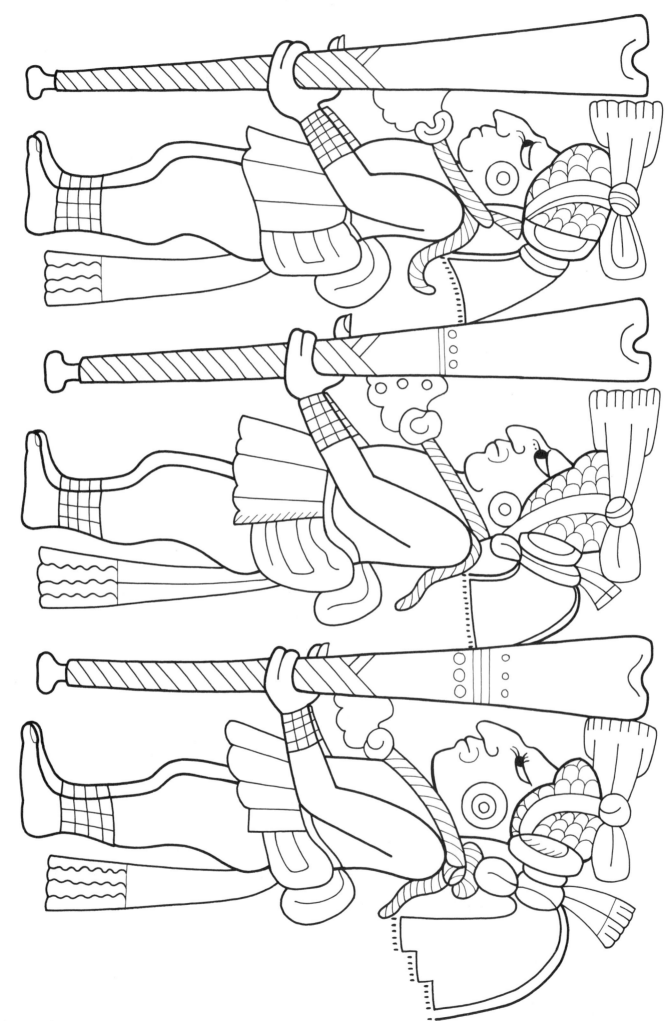

PADDLERS OF THE GENTLEMAN FROM RATINLINXUL

The merchant travelled in boats such as that shown on the inside front cover.

From a painted vase from Ratinlinxul, Guatemala highlands; University Museum, Philadelphia. Late Classic period, Chama 3, A.D. 750–900.

From a fragment of a painted vase from Actun Balam Cave, Cayo District, British Honduras. Late Classic period, 7th century A.D.

A MAYA LADY TRAVELLING

From a Maya painted dish from Yuca-
tan; Private Collection, Mexico City.
Late Classic–Early Postclassic period,
A.D. 850-1100.

A MAYA PRIEST

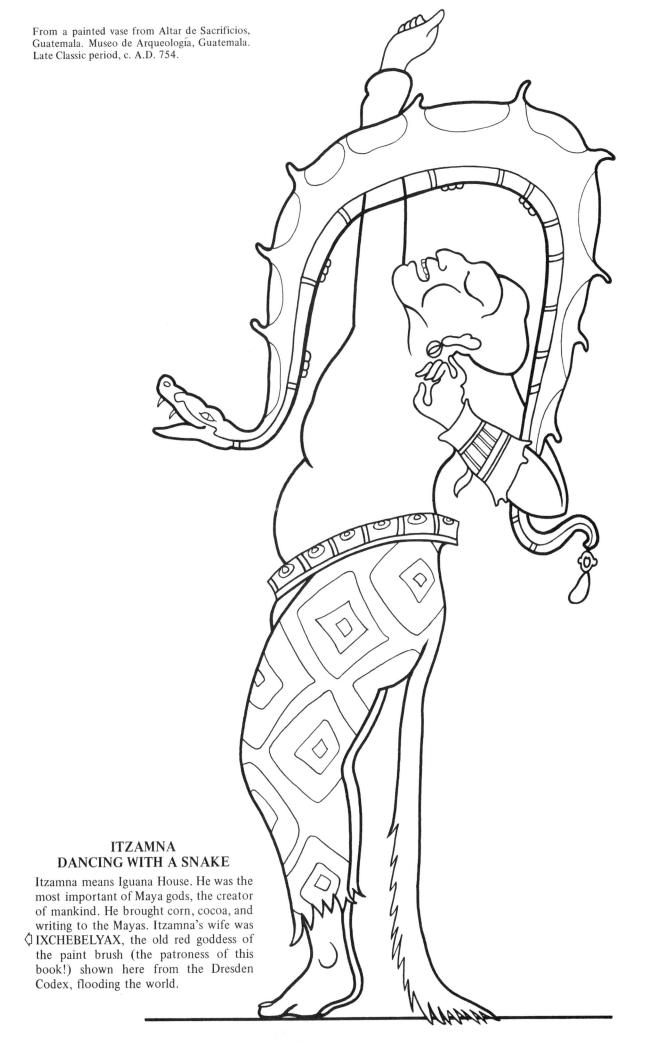

From a painted vase from Altar de Sacrificios, Guatemala. Museo de Arqueología, Guatemala. Late Classic period, c. A.D. 754.

ITZAMNA
DANCING WITH A SNAKE

Itzamna means Iguana House. He was the most important of Maya gods, the creator of mankind. He brought corn, cocoa, and writing to the Mayas. Itzamna's wife was ◊ IXCHEBELYAX, the old red goddess of the paint brush (the patroness of this book!) shown here from the Dresden Codex, flooding the world.

From the Dresden Codex; Sächsische Landesbibliothek; style of the Classic period, A.D. 1100–1200.

YUM KAX, THE CORN GOD, RIDING ON THE BACK OF AN OPOSSUM GOD IN A NEW YEAR CELEBRATION

From the Dresden Codex, probably from
Campeche. Sächsische Landesbibliothek;
style of the Classic period, A.D. 1100-1200.

A MAYA WARRIOR WITH THE HEAD OF A JUNGLE CAT

Hundreds of Maya books existed before the Spanish conquest, but all but three were burned by
the conquerors because they contained "superstition and the devil's lies." Of the three surviving
books, or codices, the Dresden Codex is the oldest, dating from the 12th or 13th century. It is
over eleven feet long and is folded into 78 pages, and is written on paper made from the bark of
a tree. Much of it is undeciphered.

From Stela 3, Machaquila,
El Peten, Guatemala.
c. A.D. 825.

**A MAYA CHIEF HOLDING A MANIKIN
SCEPTER WHILE A FISH NIBBLES AT
THE WATER LILY ON HIS BONNET**

The water lily was a symbol of water and may have
represented the primeval lake beneath the earth.

From a damaged stela, No. 7 in Agua-
teca, El Peten, Guatemala. A.D. 800.

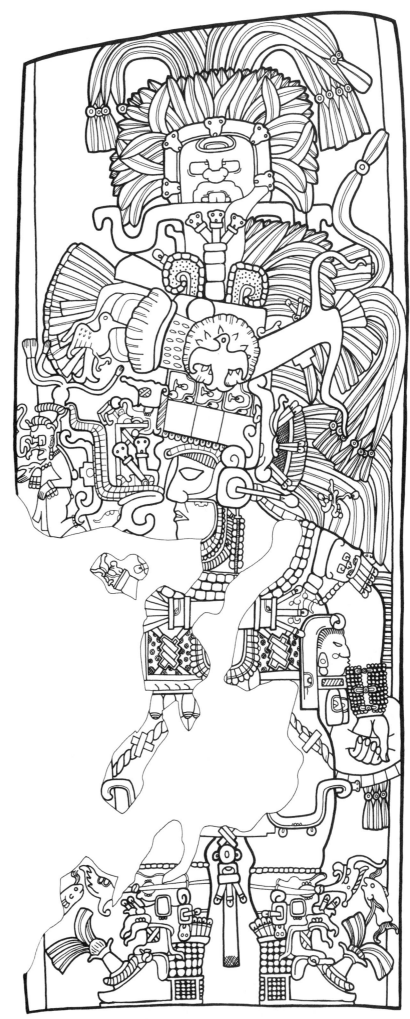

A MAYA CHIEF TO RESTORE

Some of the pieces are missing because
the stela from which this is taken was
badly damaged by time. See if you can
restore the missing lines; the picture
opposite is somewhat similar.

A MASKED NOBLEMAN AT BONAMPAK WITH TWO TRUMPETERS

Bonampak, Maya for "painted walls," was discovered in 1946 by a young American explorer in the jungles of southern Mexico. There remain many things yet to discover in Mayan archaeology.

From the murals at Bonampak, Chiapas, Mexico. Classic period, c. A.D. 700.

A STERN MAYA CHIEF AT BONAMPAK

He is dressed in a jaguar skin, a sign of his rank.

From the Dresden Codex;
Sächsische Landesbibliothek;
style of the Classic period,
A.D. 1100-1200.

KUKULCAN, THE FOUNDER OF CIVILIZATION AND THE BUILDER OF CITIES

Kukulcan was an exiled Toltec king from Tula, in Central Mexico, who had been forced to leave due to the evil magic of Tezcatlipoca. He brought his people in boats to Chichen Itzá about A.D. 987. He was a good and just leader, and accordingly, he became a god. Kukulcan II founded the city of Mayapan.

From a Capador pottery
vessel from Copán, Honduras,
7th century A.D. Peabody
Museum, Harvard University.

A MAYA DANCER

A TOLTEC CHIEF CHASING MAYA WARRIORS

From a gold disk from the Well of Sacrifice, Chichén Itzá. Peabody Museum, Harvard University.

From the Dresden Codex;
Sächsische Landesbibliothek;
style of the Classic period,
A.D. 1100-1200.

CHAC, THE RAIN GOD

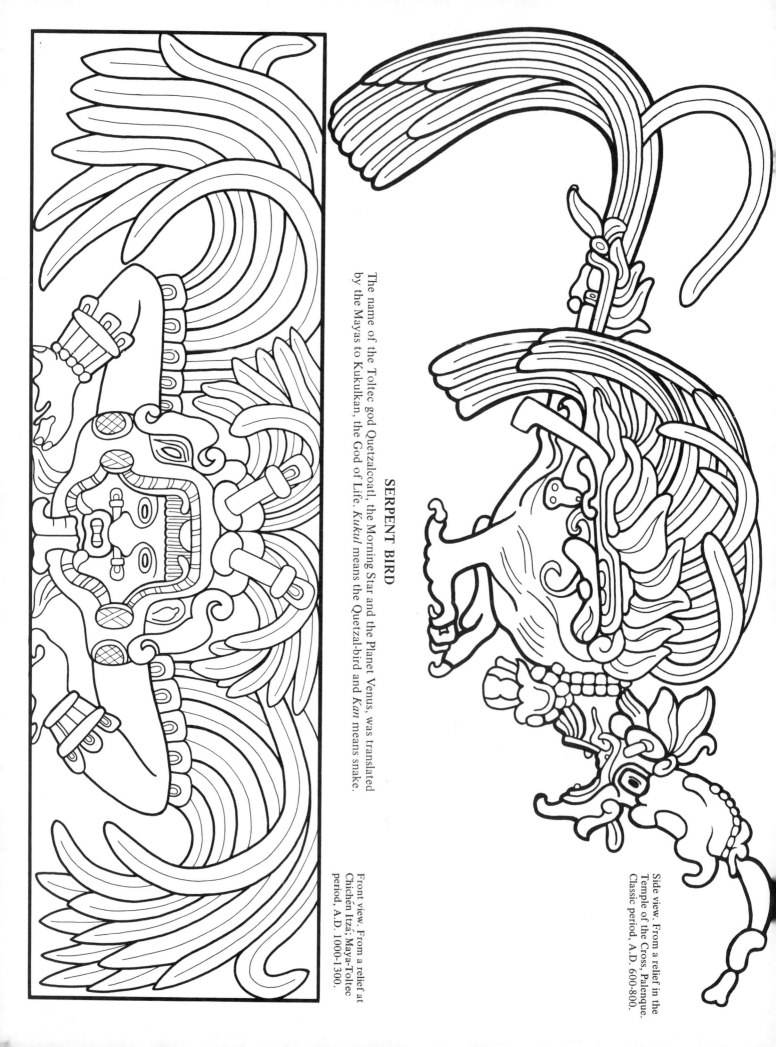

SERPENT BIRD

The name of the Toltec god Quetzalcoatl, the Morning Star and the Planet Venus, was translated by the Mayas to Kukulkan, the God of Life. *Kukul* means the Quetzal-bird and *Kan* means snake.

Front view. From a relief at Chichén Itzá; Maya-Toltec period, A.D. 1000–1300.

Side view. From a relief in the Temple of the Cross, Palenque. Classic period, A.D. 600–800.

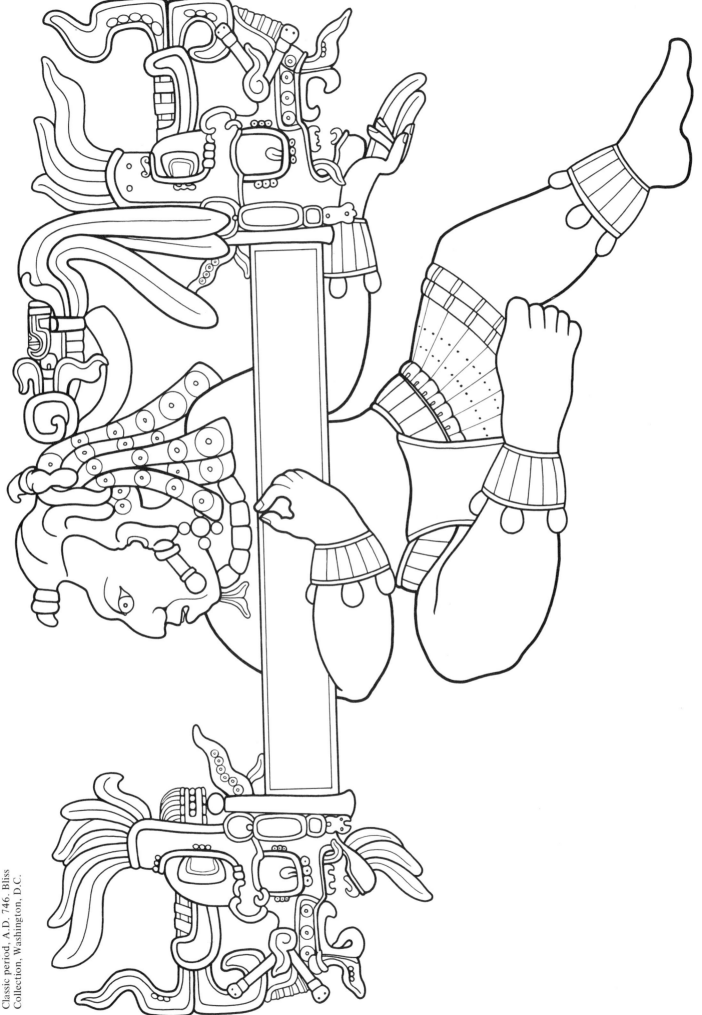

From a limestone lintel from Kuná, Chiapas, Mexico. Late Classic period, A.D. 746. Bliss Collection, Washington, D.C.

From Stela H, Copán, Honduras, A.D. 782.

From a lintel of carved sapodilla
wood from Temple IV, Tikal, Peten,
Guatemala. Classic period, c. A.D.
747. Museum für Völkerkunde, Basle.

A MAYA LADY

Copán is famous for its 38
beautiful stelas, thought to be
portraits of great people. Only
Stela H is a representation of
a female.

**A GREAT MAYA RULER OF
TIKAL ON HIS THRONE** ⟡

The earliest known dated Maya in-
scription, from A.D. 292, was found
at Tikal in 1959 on a stela numbered
29. Tikal is probably the oldest center
of Maya civilization, and has six great
pyramid-temples which are the high-
est buildings in the Maya territory.
Temple IV is 229 feet tall.

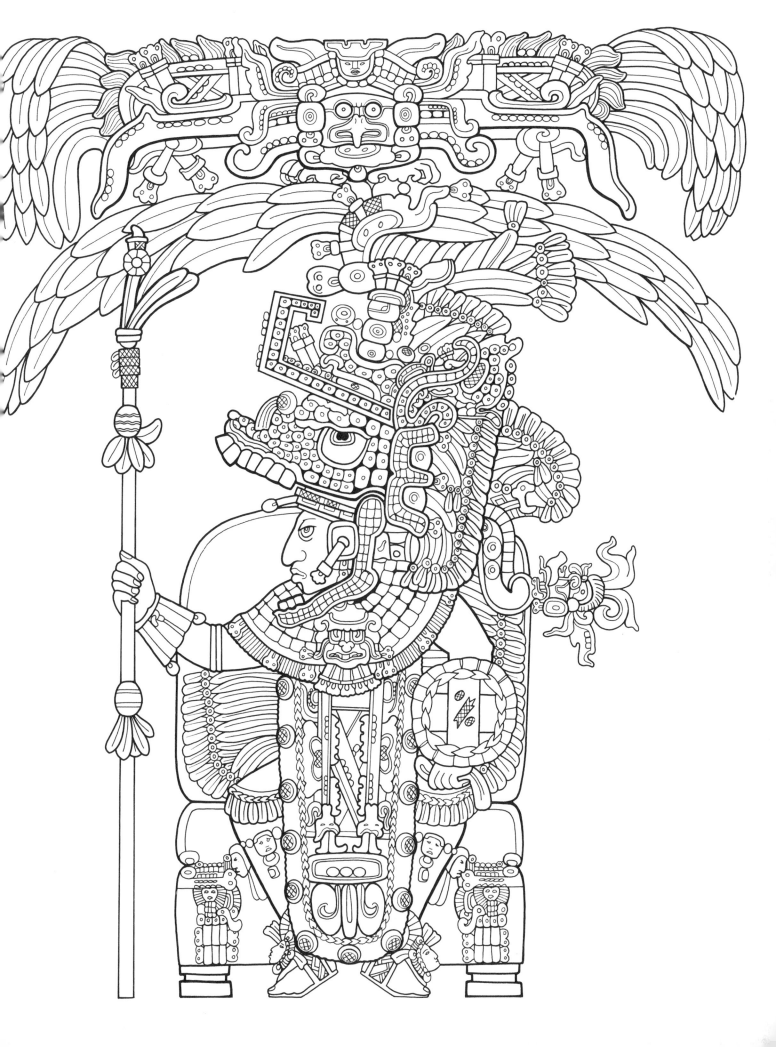

From the Dresden Codex;
Sächsische Landesbibliothek;
style of the Classic period,
A.D. 1100-1200.

**EKCHUAH, THE OLD BLACK GOD OF WAR, PROTECTOR OF MERCHANTS
AND GOD OF THE COCOA PLANT, WHOSE BEANS WERE USED AS MONEY**

From a Maya stone marker from a ball court, from Cancuén, Guatemala lowlands; Museo Nacional de Arqueología, Guatemala. Late Classic period, c. A.D. 795.

TWO BALL PLAYERS

The game of Tlachtli was played with a six inch rubber ball and was based on the movements of the moon and stars. The game represented the struggle between Xolotl, the god of twilight and the setting sun, and Quetzalcoatl, the god of the morning star and the rising sun. It represented the struggle between light and darkness and the changes of fate. The ball court had a temple at each end and there were stone rings along the walled sides through which the ball was meant to pass. Jewelry was piled at each end of the court and wagers were made. The players could bounce the ball only with their hips, which were padded, often with stone yokes. Whichever side put the ball through the ring first won the game and the jewelry. Omens were read by the movements of the ball.

From a polychrome vase from
Cahuachi, Nazca, Peru. Museum
für Völkerkunde, Munich.

A Spanish edition of this book will be available soon.
Tendremos muy pronto una edición de este libro en español.